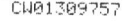

THE ULTIMATE MEN'S BOOK OF BEER

AN ENTERTAINING GUIDE TO THE WORLD'S GREATEST BEVERAGE

©PINK RHINO PRESS 2024. ALL RIGHTS RESERVED

Welcome to The Ultimate Men's Book of Beer

Greetings, beer fans and enthusiasts!

If you've ever found yourself gazing lovingly at a pint of beer, engaged in a passionate debate over the merits of a favourite ale. Or enjoying the simple camaraderie of a pub night with your buddies; then this book is your frothy ticket to beer lover's heaven.

During life's sweet adventure, few pleasures match the sheer, unbridled joy of sipping a cold one with pals.

Whether you're a seasoned beer connoisseur or a just a lover of a casual pint with friends, we've crafted this book as the ultimate guide to all thing's beer. From the delightful to the downright outrageous, we've wrapped it all up with a lavish bow of humour and entertainment.

From the basics of brewing to quirky beer facts. From beer games that'll turn your evening into a riot to a chart of the world's most prodigious beer drinking countries; this book has got it all.

Have you ever wondered how to tell a wheat beer from a pilsner or how to rule the beer pong table? This book has the answers you need.

Plus, we'll take you on a tour of beer festivals that'll make your taste buds tingle and introduce you to beer adventures that go beyond the barstool.

So, grab your favourite brew, crack it open, and let's dive into a world where every sip is a smile, every laugh is a toast, and every page is a ticket to beer-soaked bliss.

Cheers!

This book is dedicated to Henry, Tilly, Rafe and my long-suffering wife Becky.

You make life and beer all the better.

To all those I've shared a beer with I say 'Cheers!'

It's your round next....

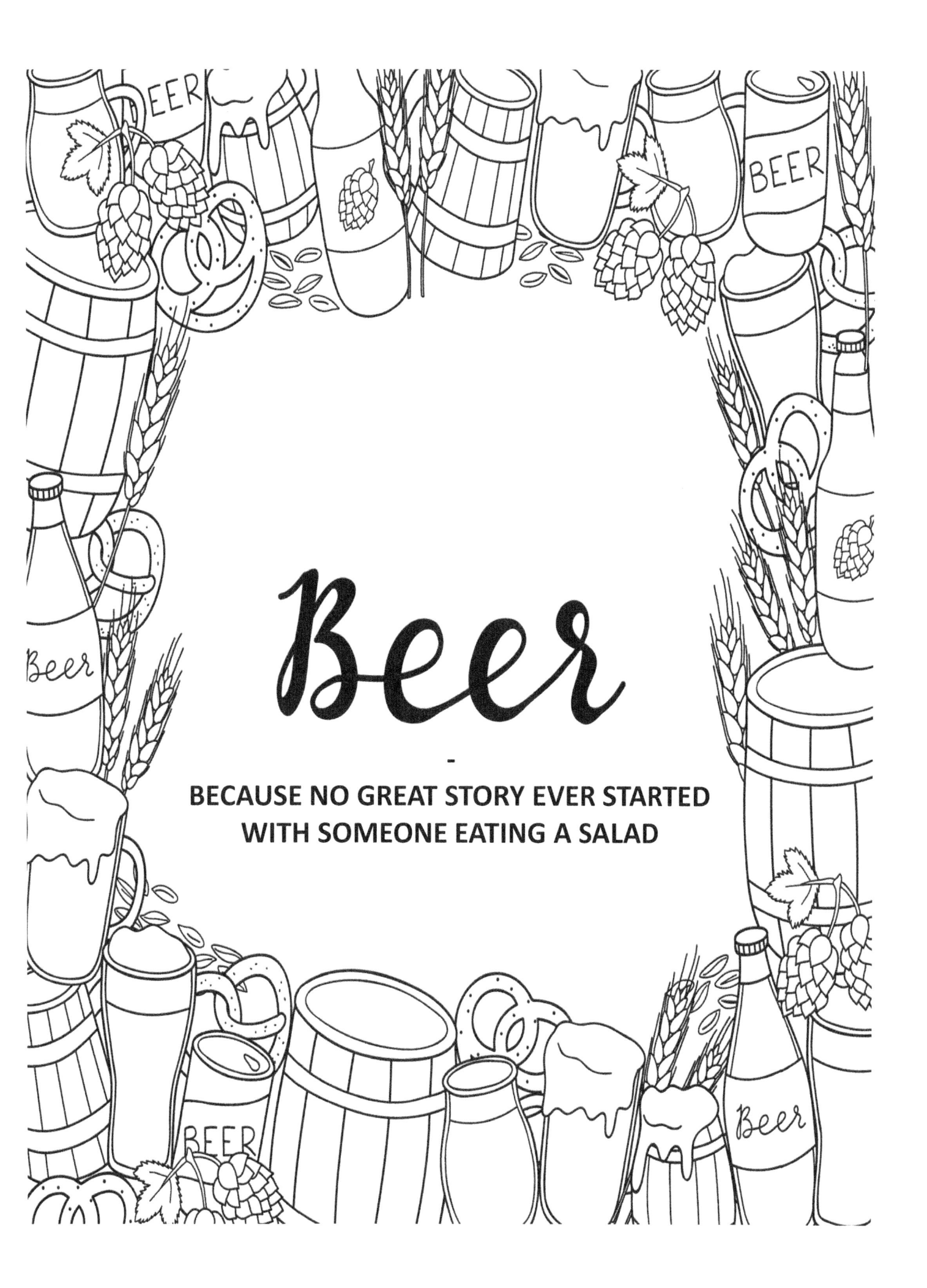

Beer

BECAUSE NO GREAT STORY EVER STARTED
WITH SOMEONE EATING A SALAD

The Beer Drinking Commandments

Before we go forth on our beer guzzling adventure, it's important to take heed of the following beer drinking commandments. The code by which we should all strive to live by:

1. Thou shalt never waste good beer — the nectar of the gods is there to be savoured and celebrated!

2. Always embrace the 'Beer Geek' within - nerding out over hop varieties is not only allowed but encouraged.

3. Do not be a monogamous beer drinker - exploring uncharted beer territories is like embarking on a liquid adventure. Your new favourite tipple could be waiting just around the corner!

4. When in doubt, go local - supporting local breweries is like giving a high-five to your taste buds.

5. Thou shalt never drink beer containing cocktail umbrellas or fruit slices as accessories — we're men, not salad enthusiasts!

6. Thou shall not chug craft beer like a frat party - savour each sip, and let those flavours dance on your tongue.

7. Always remember, beer is a social lubricant - it turns awkward moments into hilarious memories!

8. Thou shall not engage in beer debates during the big game - because sport and beer go together like hops and barley.

9. Thou shalt not judge others for their beer preferences - unless they dare to disrespect the holy IPA!

10. Always respect the bartender - they hold the keys to beer utopia, and a well-tipped bartender is a friend for life!

11. Thou shall not use beer as a performance-enhancing potion - unless, of course, you're competing in a beer mile!

12. Remember, beer is about enjoyment, not competition - unless you're competing to have the most fun. Then go for gold, my beer drinking brethren!

THE DOCTOR SAID JUST ONE GLASS OF BEER A DAY.

I CAN LIVE WITH THAT.

Beer

(noun)

1. *An alcoholic beverage made from yeast fermented malt, flavoured with hops*
2. *Proof that God loves us*
3. *A source of bad decisions and good stories*
4. *Magic water for fun people*

A Frothy Tale: The Brief History of Beer - Part One

Ah, beer! The beloved beverage that has been delighting our taste buds for centuries. But do you know the fascinating story behind this foamy concoction?

Strap on your beer goggles, because we're about to embark on a side-splitting historical journey through the world of beer. Let us raise our glasses and dive headfirst into the frothy depths of beer's hilarious past.

Part 1: The Ancient Brewing Chronicles

Around 4,000 BCE, ancient civilisations in Mesopotamia began cultivating grain, eventually leading to the creation of beer. These early brewers, who were often highly respected priestesses, held the power of turning barley into liquid gold. Archaeologists linked ceramic tablets with the famous 'Hymn to Ninkasi' — a prayer to the Sumerian goddess of beer from this period. Can you imagine beer as a holy beverage? Talk about divine intervention!

Part 2: Beer Through the Ages

Fast forward to the Middle Ages, where monasteries became the epicentres of brewing knowledge. Monks dedicated themselves to perfecting the art of brewing, showing that devotion and good taste go hand in hand. Beer became a staple of daily life, as it was considered a safer alternative to water (and much more enjoyable, if you ask me!).

Part 3: A Leap of Faith

The 16th century saw the rise of hops in beer brewing, which added a bitter yet tantalising flavour. This revolution in brewing technique led to the creation of India Pale Ale (IPA), igniting an obsession that continues today.

Part 4: Beer Revolution!

With the arrival of the Industrial Revolution in the 18th century came steam power, and with it, the mass production of beer. Breweries began popping up faster than you could say, "Cheers!" This era witnessed the birth of iconic beer styles like Pilsner and Stout, offering beer lovers a greater selection of choice.

CONFUCIUS SAYS, "BEAUTY IS IN THE EYE OF THE BEER HOLDER"

The Anatomy of a Beer Drinker

Ah, the humble beer drinker. Thee whose taste buds dance in delight at the mere sight of a frothy pint. Let us explore the beer-drinker's body parts and their uproarious involvement in the glorious act of beer consumption.

The Frothy Forehead

As you take that refreshing first sip, the forehead may glisten and sparkle; but fear not! It's merely the beer angels granting their blessing.

The Bubbly Brain

The control centre that steers the beer drinker's voyage. Conjuring the finest banter and "ingenious" ideas after just a few pints.

The Malt Munchers (Taste Buds)

These tiny flavour connoisseurs sit proudly on your tongue, doing the beer-tasting tango with each sip. They have a knack for deciphering complex brews and always ask for an encore!

The Gassy Guffaw

The beer-drinker's laughter! After a few rounds, it echoes like the claps of a 1,000 beer loving angels!

The Hoppy Heart

This courageous organ beats with the rhythm of a beer-fuelled anthem, pumping liquid courage through your veins. It's the cheerleader that says, "Go on, have another one! No regrets!"

The Beloved Beer Belly (Paunch of Pride)

A badge of honour! This proud protuberance is like a soft, jiggly trophy shelf. Showcasing the memories of countless brewery visits, beer festivals, and late-night bonding sessions with your fellow beer enthusiasts. It's a living testament to the motto, "In beer, we trust!"

The Ale-elbows

These trusty joints help you maintain your drinking posture through those marathon sessions at the bar. Just don't lean too heavily, lest you become a fixture!

The Hops-n-Hips

These gyrating hipsters are the life of the beer party. Their snake like rotations dance into gear whether you're busting moves on the dance floor or manoeuvring around barstools.

The Lager Legs

These staunch pillars of defiance keep you steady, even after one too many. When others wobble, your lager legs remain firm; defying the laws of physics.

The Mighty Grasp

The beer drinker's hands develop vice like grips that never let go of their precious beer glass cargo!

Sixth Sense: The Beer-dar

A unique gift possessed only by seasoned beer drinkers. It helps you locate the nearest pub or brewery within a 10-mile radius.

A DAY WITHOUT BEER PROBABLY WOULDN'T KILL ME

BUT WHY TAKE THE RISK?

IT'S BEER O'CLOCK!!!

Do you like to go for a swift half? Are you planning to get tiddly or fancy a couple of drinky winkys? However you describe your intention for a few beers, you can't beat the coded creativity of a good euphemism for getting drunk.

Next time you head for a beer, enter the sweet gates of inebriation armed with plenty of ways to describe your drunken state! From the polite to the inventive, here are some of our favourites.

- Getting wankered
- Pissed up
- Three sheets to the wind
- Getting hammered
- Tired and emotional
- Trollied
- Legless
- Blotto
- Wasted
- Cock-eyed
- Under the influence
- Steaming
- Bladdered
- Well oiled
- Mullered
- Rat arsed
- Bevved up
- Drunk as a skunk
- Pissed as a fart

Name 5 more of your favourites below:

1. ....
2. ....
3. ....
4. ....
5. ....

When my friend feel asleep at the bar, I poured my beer on him.
It was a brewed awakening.

Types of Drunk People

'Every man is many men' said someone wise once. And there's nothing quite like a few beers to bring out some unique characteristics in your fellow drinking buddies.

Which category do you fit into? Here are 10 types of drunk people to watch out for at the bar!

The Superhero Drunk

When this guy hits the bottle, he instantly believes he possesses extraordinary powers. He may strut around the bar wearing a makeshift cape (probably made from a tablecloth) and take on dare devil challenges from all onlookers. He might attempt to fly off a bar stool or challenge the jukebox to a dance-off. Just pray he doesn't try to save you from your drink!

The Philosophical Drunk

This deep-thinking drinker can turn even the most casual conversation into a profound existential debate. As soon as the alcohol hits his system, he'll wax lyrical about the meaning of life, the universe, and why they invented flavoured vodka. Be prepared for a night of pondering the mysteries of the universe over pints.

The Dancing Machine

This guy doesn't just dance; he becomes one with the music. As soon as the DJ drops a funky beat, he'll bust out moves you didn't know were humanly possible. Whether it's breakdancing or the robot, he'll own the dance floor and leave everyone in awe. Just make sure to give him some space, or you might catch an accidental elbow to the face.

The Emotional Drunk

When this person gets a few drinks in, their emotions go into overdrive. They'll go from laughing hysterically to sobbing uncontrollably within seconds. They'll hug strangers, profess their love to the bartender, and probably start apologising for things they did in elementary school. Keep a tissue handy, because you might need to offer a sympathetic shoulder.

The Expert Storyteller

This guy has a story for every occasion, and he's determined to share them all when he's had a few. From epic fishing tales to improbable encounters with celebrities, his stories will have you on the edge of your barstool, simultaneously entertained and questioning their authenticity. Just nod, smile and enjoy the wild ride.

The Karaoke King

Once the karaoke machine is fired up, this guy transforms into a superstar. Armed with a microphone and a belly full of liquid courage, he'll belt out power ballads like a seasoned pro. Watch out for his rendition of "Livin' on a Prayer" or "Bohemian Rhapsody"—it might just blow the roof off the joint. And don't be surprised if he starts taking song requests from the bar staff.

The Inappropriate Comedian

This person's humour becomes cranked up to 11 after a few drinks. They'll crack jokes that are so hilariously inappropriate you won't know whether to laugh or cringe. From risqué one-liners to punchlines that push the boundaries of good taste, their comedic timing is spot on... even if their material might make your grandma blush.

The Liquid GPS

No matter how many bars you visit, this guy always knows where the next one is. With his internal compass calibrated to guide him from pub to pub, he's like a living GPS for the best watering holes in town. Just follow his lead, and you'll end up in the promised land of good beer and fun times.

The Drunken Food Critic

When this person indulges in a few drinks, they develop an unmatched palate for bar food. Suddenly, they're able to discern the subtle nuances of every deep-fried delicacy on the menu. Expect detailed analyses of chicken wings, debates about the proper amount of cheese on nachos, and eloquent odes to the perfect jalapeño pepper.

The Uncoordinated Dancer

This individual has the unfortunate habit of turning into a marionette with tangled strings as soon as they start dancing. Their limbs flail about with a complete disregard for rhythm, making their dance moves resemble a bizarre interpretive dance routine. It's best to give them a wide berth to avoid any accidental collisions.

I'M NOT AS THINK...

AS YOU DRUNK I AM

▲

SWIPE UP

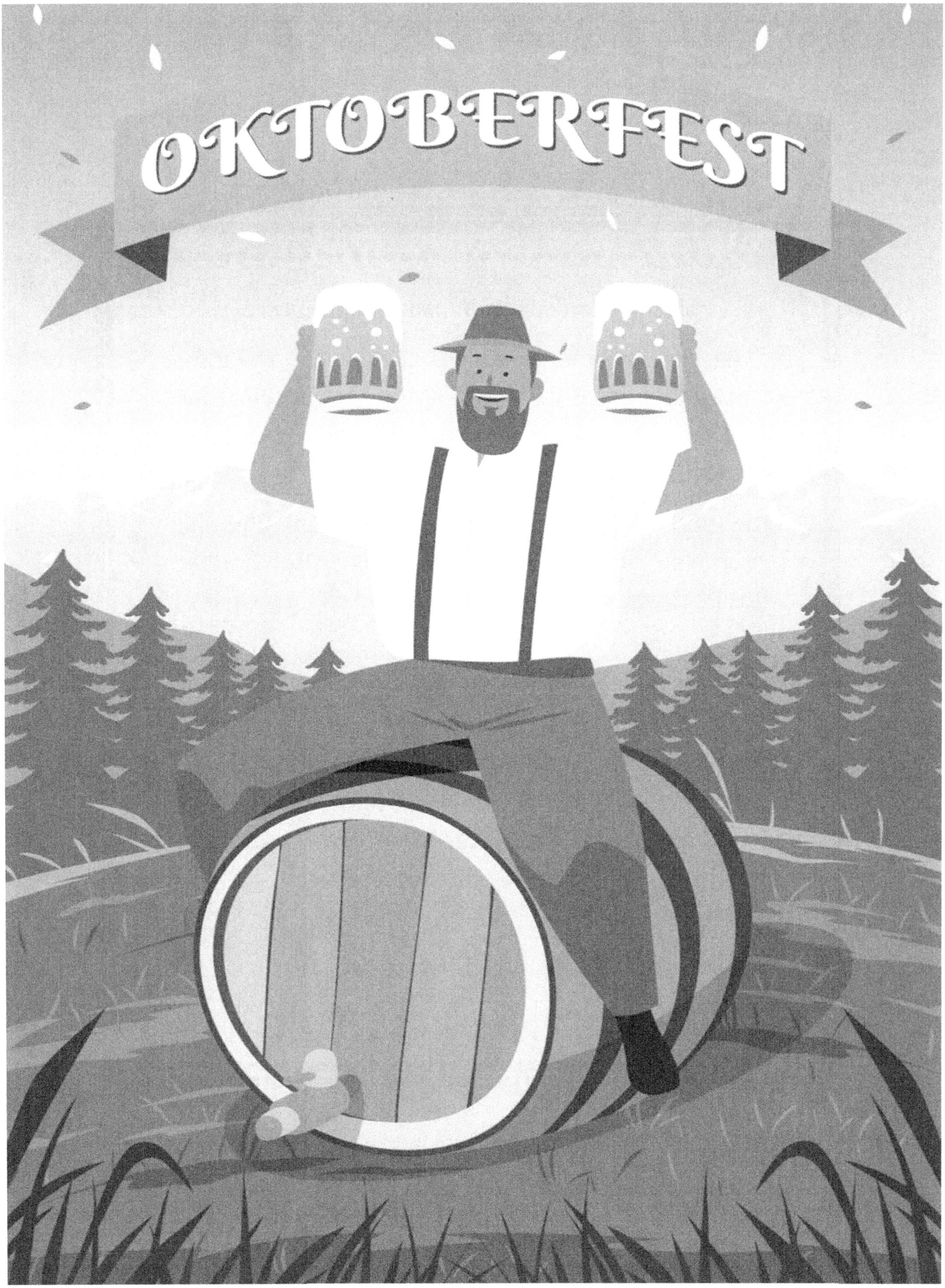
OKTOBERFEST

Sir Winston's Wild Whiskey Adventure

Legend has it that one night during World War II, the illustrious British Prime Minister, Sir Winston Churchill, had a few too many sips of whiskey.

In a state of inebriation, he decided it was high time to visit the Royal Air Force's headquarters. Churchill stumbled into the building, wearing a siren helmet upside down on his head and brandishing a cigar as his weapon of choice.

Completely oblivious to his dishevelled appearance, he demanded an update on the war effort, slurring his words and causing confusion among the officers. It took a while for them to realize the man they were dealing with was none other than their beloved Prime Minister.

Needless to say, the next morning, Churchill woke up with a killer hangover and a sheepish grin on his face.

Beer World Records – Part 1

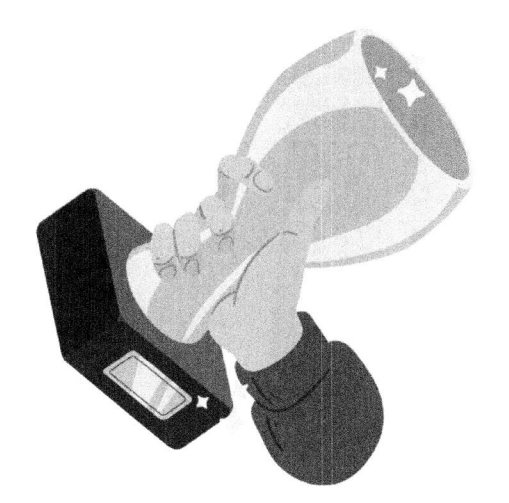

The current Guinness world record for the fastest time taken to drink a pint of beer is just over 1.6 seconds by Peter Dowdeswell of the UK!

The largest beer festival in the world is Oktoberfest in Munich, Germany. The festival attracts over 6 million visitors every year, who enjoy live music, Bavarian cuisine and of course, lots of German beer!

The largest number of commercially available beer stands at 2004 varieties at the Delirium Café in Brussels, Belgium. More than enough to keep beer enthusiasts busy for a day or two!

Alcohol is never the answer...

But it's a good way of forgetting the question!

The Eighth Wonder of the World

The famed wrestler and actor Andre the Giant – known as the Eighth Wonder of the World – was by all accounts a big character and an even bigger drinker! Unofficially crowned 'the greatest drunk on Earth', here are some of his legendary drinking exploits.*

Andre once drank 119 12-oz beers in six hours! That equated to one beer every 3 minutes for six hours.

Andre rang up a $40,000 bar tab at the Hyatt in London. His favourite order was an 'American' – a pitcher filled with 40oz of various liquors.

Drank a case of 12 bottles of strong French wine in 3 hours!

Once drank a plane's entire stock of vodka on a flight to Japan!

*Don't try this at home. Andre the Giant was 7'4" and weighed over 500 pounds!

A Frothy Tale: The Brief History of Beer - Part Two

Part 5: Prohibition Blues

Through the evolution of beer to the present day, sadly not all was laughter and clinking glasses. The early 20th century was marked by the dark age of Prohibition, when the U.S. government tried to dampen the spirits of beer lovers. In 1920, bars closed, beer became illegal, and America's collective beer belly went into hibernation. Thank goodness that nightmare didn't last and was overturned in 1933!

Part 6: The Rise of Craft Beer

In the late 20th century, a new movement bubbled up: craft beer. Small, independent breweries began experimenting with flavours and techniques, creating a dizzying variety of brews. Suddenly, beer drinkers had more choices than a kid in a sweet shop. The craft beer revolution reinvigorated the world of beer, inspiring beer snobs and aficionados alike to seek out the next big thing on the beer brewing scene.

Part 7: Beer in the Digital Age

With the dawn of the internet, beer enthusiasts found their virtual paradise. Online forums, beer-rating apps, and social media groups brought beer lovers together like never before. The virtual beer community boomed, sharing recommendations, funny beer memes, and hilarious mishaps that can only happen after a few too many pints. Let's raise a glass to beer memes and virtual camaraderie!

Conclusion

From its divine origins to the craft beer renaissance, beer has woven its way into the hearts, minds, and bellies of men who appreciate its historical and satisfying charm. So, my fellow beer-loving brethren, let's raise our glasses and toast to the foamy alcoholic beverage that has stood the test of time. Cheers to beer, laughter, and the jolly journeys it takes us on!

BEER

IT'S LIKE POURING SMILES ON YOUR BRAIN

BEER TRIVIA

Beer dates back over 4,000 years with the oldest known recipe dating from ancient Mesopotamia (modern day Iran.)

The strongest beer ever made was called 'Snake Venom', which had an alcohol content stronger than most spirits at 67.5% ABV (alcohol by volume.)

In 1814, a huge beer flood took place in London when a brewery's fermenting vat ruptured. This caused a tidal wave of beer to flood the streets and kill eight people.

In the Czech Republic – the country with the world's largest consumption per person – beer is often cheaper than bottled water.

Beer is the most popular alcoholic beverage in the world with over 50 billion gallons consumed globally every year. It is also the third most consumed drink overall behind tea and water.

Prohibition in the US occurred between 1920 and 1933. It lasted 13 years, 10 months and 19 days. But whose counting?

BEER MATHS

ONE BEER

A COUPLE OF BEERS

A FEW BEERS

15 REASONS WHY BEER IS BETTER THAN WOMEN

1. When you go to a bar, you can always pick up a beer
2. A beer won't get jealous if you grab another beer
3. You can have more than one beer and not feel guilty
4. A beer is always wet
5. A frigid beer is a good beer
6. A beer never has a headache
7. Beer is never late
8. A beer always goes down easy
9. Hangovers are temporary
10. Beer can be enjoyed all month long
11. You can watch sports all day with a beer
12. If you pour a beer right, you're guaranteed to get good head
13. You'll never have to wine and dine a beer
14. A beer doesn't get upset if you come home with another beer
15. Beer can be shared with your friends

Hey, stop hogging all the beer...

You're being shellfish!

It was the booze talking!

Match the quotes and draw a line to the famous person that said them (answers below)!

1. "I feel sorry for people who don't drink. When they wake up in the morning, that's as good as they're going to feel all day."

2. "I'm on a whiskey diet. I've lost three days already."

3. "Beer, if drunk in moderation, softens the temper, cheers the spirit, and promotes health."

4. "You're not drunk if you can lie on the floor without holding on."

5. "I work until beer o'clock."

- Thomas Jefferson
- Dean Martin
- Stephen King
- Frank Sinatra
- Tommy Cooper

Answers: 1 = Frank Sinatra 2 = Tommy Cooper 3 = Thomas Jefferson 4 = Dean Martin 5 = Stephen King

The Beer Drinking Champions League

Did you make the list?

Here are the top beer drinking countries from around the world!

1. Czech Republic – The Pilsner Paradise

Taking the top spot with a per capita consumption of 142 litres, the Czech's take their beer seriously. They even have a beer spa where you can bathe in beer while sipping on your favourite brew!

2. Germany – Oktoberfest Legends

In second place, the Germans guzzle a hearty 110 litres per capita. Fun fact: Germany is synonymous with Oktoberfest, where they celebrate beer with wild abandon. Over 7 million litres of beer are guzzled during this legendary event.

3. Austria - Beyond the Alps, It's Beer Time

Consuming a solid 108 litres per person, in Austria, beer gardens are a way of life. Lounging under shady trees, sipping your favourite tipple, and enjoying the company of good friends. Amen!

4. Poland - A Spirited Brewing Culture

Swigging a refreshing 99 litres per person every year. The Polish love their beer so much that they host the "Festival of Good Beer," where you can sample over 250 different varieties.

5. Ireland – Guinness Galore

The Irish chug away approx. 96 litres per person! Fun Fact: Ireland's famed stout Guinness is not just a beer; it's a cultural icon! They even have a Guinness World Records Museum in Dublin, celebrating both the beer and the wacky world of records.

ANNUAL PER CAPITA BEER CONSUMPTION (LITRES PER PERSON)

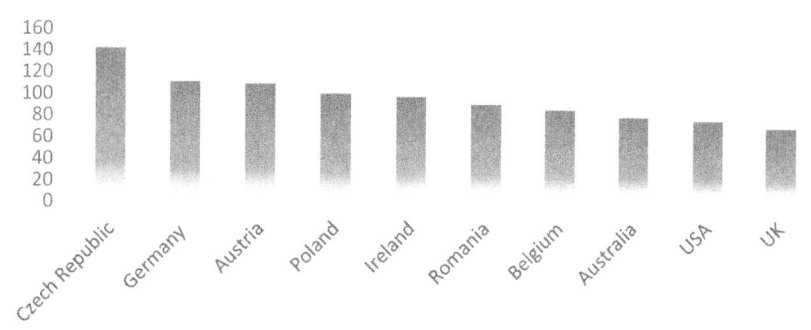

Country	Litres
Czech Republic	~142
Germany	~110
Austria	~108
Poland	~99
Ireland	~96
Romania	~89
Belgium	~84
Australia	~77
USA	~74
UK	~67

6. Romania - The Beer Renaissance

With a spirited 89 litres per person, Romania is experiencing a beer renaissance, with craft breweries popping up like mushrooms after rain. They're embracing their brewing traditions with a modern twist, delighting beer enthusiasts across the land.

7. Belgium - The Beer Paradise

In 7th place, the Belgium's consume a staggering 84 litres per person. Fun fact: Belgium is a beer lover's wonderland with a beer for every occasion, boasting over 1,600 unique beer varieties!

8. Australia – Brews & BBQs

In Australia, beer and barbecues go hand in hand with a cool 77 litres per person consumed every year. Their love for "barbies" and brews makes them masters of the outdoor party scene.

9. United States - Land of Craft Beer

Consuming a refreshing 74 litres per person, the United States is a craft beer paradise, with over 8,000 breweries scattered across the country. From IPAs to stouts, they've got a beer style for every taste bud!

10. United Kingdom - A Pint of Tradition

In 10th place with a jolly good 67 litres per person, the UK's beer culture is deeply rooted in tradition. They even have "Beer Day Britain," a nationwide celebration of all thing's beer, raising a toast to their beloved beverage.

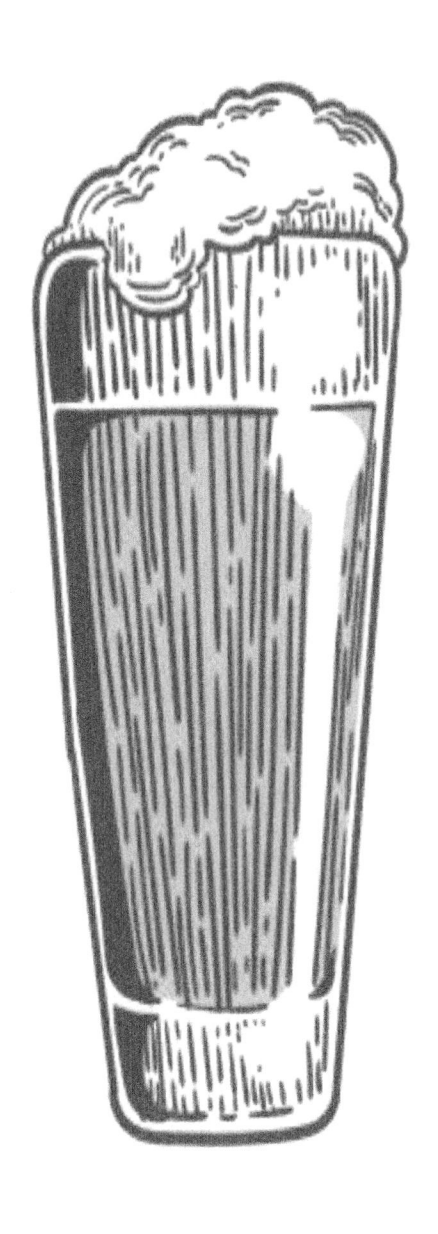

THE AVERAGE MAN WALKS AROUND 1200 MILES A YEAR, AND DRINKS 28 GALLONS OF BEER.

THAT MEANS THE AVERAGE MAN GETS 42 MILES TO THE GALLON. NOT BAD AT ALL.

The Idiots Guide to Making Beer

Welcome to the wonderful world of beer brewing; your window into how this glorious drink is made and where your creative prowess can flow like the beer tap on a Friday night.

If you've ever wondered what it takes to create your own liquid gold, then rest your pints gently for a second gentleman. We've created this brief guide just for you.

So grab your sense of adventure, a few essential tools, and let's get brewing!

First things first:

Before embarking on this thirst-quenching quest, you'll need some basic equipment. Don't worry, you won't need a PhD in nuclear physics or a fancy laboratory.

Here's a simple checklist to get you started:

- A large stainless-steel pot for boiling the ingredients.
- A fermenter (a food-grade plastic bucket or glass demijohn) – this is where the magic happens!
- Airlocks and stoppers to keep everything sealed and happy.
- A hydrometer to measure specific gravity (SG) and track your beer's progress.
- A thermometer to ensure you're brewing at the right temperature.
- A racking cane and siphon for transferring your brew.
- Bottles or kegs to house the final product.
- And, of course, your ingredients! Malt extract, hops, yeast, and water will become your new best friends.

Choose Your Beer Adventure

It's time to decide what style of beer you want to brew. Do you have a passion for a hoppy IPA, a malty stout, or a crisp pilsner? Each style has its own unique characteristics and ingredients. Pick one that suits your taste or throw caution to the wind and create your own brew hybrid!

The Brewing Process

1. Sanitise, Sanitise, Sanitise: Remember - cleanliness is next to beerliness! Make sure all equipment is thoroughly clean and sanitised to prevent any pesky bacteria from crashing your home brew party.

2. Steep and Boil: For extract brewing, start by steeping specialty grains in hot water for around 30 minutes at 150-170 Fahrenheit (65-75 degrees Celsius) to extract their flavours. Then, bring the liquid to the boil and add your malt extract. Embrace the steamy goodness and stir it like a cackling witch tending her cauldron until it all dissolves.

3. Hop Time: Let's hop to it! Hops can be added at different intervals during the boil to control the bitterness, flavour, and aroma. It's your choice whether you cast them in with abandon or place gently with tweezers. Just don't forget; hops are the spice of beer life!

4. Time to Chill: Once your boil is complete, it's time to take away the heat and cool your wort down. Use an ice bath, a wort chiller, or even your trusty snowman-shaped ice cubes. The goal? Bring your tasty new creation down to a temperature where your yeast won't be scared to party.

5. In Yeast We Trust: It's time to add your yeast to the wort and watch the fermentation magic happen. Like inviting a group of beer swigging single celled teenagers with rampaging hormones to the party, these guys will transform sugar into alcohol. Just keep a close eye on them and ensure the temperature is just right for the action to start.

What is the definition of a balanced diet? A beer in each hand.

6. Patience is a Virtue: It's time to take your foot off the gas pedal and relax. Fermentation takes time, my friend. Relax, have a beer (preferably not the one you're brewing), and let nature do its thing. Depending on the beer style and yeast strain, this can take anywhere from a couple of weeks to a few months. Be patient and remember that good things come to those who wait.

7. It's Time for the Bubbles: Once fermentation is complete, the next step is to carbonate your beer. You can either prime your bottles with a bit of sugar or use a CO_2 system if you're kegging. Carbonation adds that delightful fizz, making your beer sparkle like a disco ball.

The Final Sip:

Congratulations, you've brewed your own beer! Now comes the fun part—tasting and sharing your creation with friends and fellow beer enthusiasts. Crack open a bottle and savour the fruits of your labour. Take note of the flavours, the aroma, and the satisfaction of knowing you created something delicious from scratch.

Remember, brewing beer is as much an art as it is a science. Don't be discouraged if your first batch isn't perfect. Like any skill worth mastering, practice makes perfect (or at least really tasty). So, keep experimenting, refine your technique, and enjoy the journey of brewing your own liquid masterpiece.

And there you have it—the Idiot's Guide to Making Beer. Now go forth, embrace your inner brewer, and let the creativity flow like a never-ending beer tap. Embrace your brewing adventures and the joy of crafting a pint of pure satisfaction!

Drink Like a Fish!

Marilyn Monroe's Tipsy Tryst

One fateful evening in the 1950s, Hollywood's iconic bombshell, Marilyn Monroe, attended a glamorous party at a luxurious mansion. As the night wore on and the drinks flowed freely, Marilyn found herself drawn to a handsome stranger. Ignoring the consequences, she suggested they sneak away to the mansion's opulent wine cellar for some privacy. Little did she know that her rendezvous would be more adventurous than anticipated. In their tipsy state, the pair stumbled upon a secret passageway that led to an underground labyrinth of interconnected wine cellars. Hours passed as they navigated the winding tunnels, growing increasingly confused and intoxicated. Finally, a butler discovered the lost duo, and the news of Marilyn's tipsy tryst quickly spread throughout Hollywood, becoming one of Tinseltown's most amusing tales.

NEVER

Look at your beer as half empty..

Look at it, as you're halfway to your NEXT BEER!

The Beer Connoisseurs Quiz

One point for each correct question answered.
See overleaf for answers.

1. What are the four main ingredients in traditional beer?
2. Which country is famous for its Oktoberfest beer festival?
3. What term is used to describe the process of converting sugars into alcohol during brewing?
4. Which beer style is known for its dark, roasted flavours with hints of coffee and chocolate?
5. What is the proper name for a beer glass with a curved shape that helps trap aromas?
6. Which beer style originated in the Czech town of Pilsen and is known for its light and crisp taste?
7. What unit is used to measure the bitterness of beer, especially in hoppy styles?
8. What is the common term for a large beer bottle that holds 1.5 litres?
9. Which gas is responsible for creating the carbonation in beer?
10. What is the term for a beer's colour, which can range from pale yellow to deep brown?
11. In which European city can you find the "Heineken Experience," a popular beer museum and brewery tour?
12. Which U.S. city hosts the Great American Beer Festival, one of the largest beer festivals in the world?
13. What is the name of the process used to remove sediment and clarify beer before bottling?
14. Which beer glass is tall, narrow, and designed to enhance the aroma of hoppy beers like IPAs?

The Beer Connoisseurs Quiz - answers

1. Water, malted barley, hops, and yeast.
2. Germany
3. Fermentation
4. Stout
5. Snifter glass
6. Pilsner
7. International Bitterness Units (IBUs)
8. Magnum
9. Carbon dioxide (CO2)
10. SRM (Standard Reference Method)
11. Amsterdam, Netherlands
12. Denver, Colorado
13. Filtration
14. Tulip glass

Why did the beer file a police report? It got mugged!

MORE BEER TRIVIA

Beer is best stored upright. Beer stored on its side is more susceptible to oxidation and contamination from the cap.

Let's drink to good health! Drinking beer could help reduce your risk of kidney stones by 40%.

The foam on top of a beer is called the 'head' and helps to release the aroma of the beer.

Beer has often been used as a form of currency and payment. Soldiers in the Roman army were given beer as a daily ration which formed part of their wages.

In 1963, Alfred Heineken introduced a beer bottle that could be used as a brick to build sustainable housing in impoverished countries.

A style of beer called 'Gose' is a wheat beer from Germany that includes additions such as salt and coriander.

Beer Festivals Around the World

Great American Beer Festival (Denver, USA): This premier beer festival takes place annually in Denver, Colorado. It showcases a vast selection of American craft beers, attracting thousands of beer enthusiasts, brewers, and industry professionals. With over 800 breweries participating, visitors get to taste a wide range of unique and innovative beers.

Oktoberfest (Munich, Germany): Possibly the most famous beer festival in the world, Oktoberfest is a grand celebration of Bavarian culture and beer. Held annually in Munich, it runs for about two weeks, usually from late September to the first weekend of October. Visitors can enjoy traditional German beer, music, dancing, and a selection of mouthwatering Bavarian delicacies.

Belgian Beer Weekend (Brussels, Belgium): Belgium is renowned for its exceptional beer, and this festival is the perfect place to sample some of the finest brews the country has to offer. Held in September, it features over 400 Belgian beers, giving attendees a chance to savour the diverse flavours and styles that Belgium is famous for.

Cambridge Beer Festival (Cambridge, UK): Organized by the Campaign for Real Ale (CAMRA), this festival held in May showcases a splendid selection of cask ales, ciders, and perries from both local and international breweries. It's a true celebration of traditional real ales and attracts beer enthusiasts from all corners of the UK.

Czech Beer Festival (Prague, Czech Republic): The Czech Republic is renowned for its long-standing beer traditions, and this festival in Prague celebrates the country's brewing heritage. Held in May, it offers an opportunity to indulge in Czech beer classics, along with traditional Czech dishes and cultural performances.

Australian International Beer Awards (Melbourne, Australia): While not a traditional festival, this beer awards event held in Melbourne is a significant global competition for brewers. It attracts entries from breweries worldwide, and the public can attend the awards presentation to enjoy a wide variety of award-winning beers.

Remember, the world of beer festivals is vast, and many other notable festivals take place in various corners of the globe. Whether you're a seasoned beer connoisseur or just a casual beer enthusiast, attending these festivals offers a delightful and unforgettable experience of the diverse and rich world of beer!

If you hold a glass of beer to your ear...

You can hear the weekend!

Beer Through the Ages: A Safer Alternative to Water

In the Middle Ages, life was far from a barrel of laughs, especially when it came to sanitation and public health. Believe it or not, beer played a crucial role in providing a safer alternative to water during this time.

1. Water Woes

The water supply during the Middle Ages was often contaminated with all sorts of unsavoury elements. Rivers, streams, and wells were polluted by human waste, animal carcasses, and various other pollutants. Drinking water directly from these sources posed a significant health risk, leading to outbreaks of waterborne diseases.

5. Social Lubricant

As beer became a staple of daily life, it also played a significant role in social gatherings and community events. In taverns and alehouses, people would come together to enjoy a pint, swap stories, and share laughter. Beer, with its slightly intoxicating effects, helped to foster a convivial atmosphere and temporarily alleviate the hardships of everyday life.

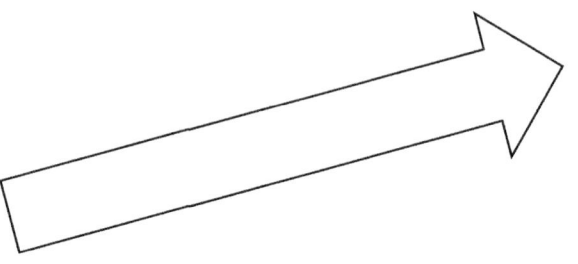

4. Nutritional Nectar

Beer in the Middle Ages was often consumed not only for its thirst-quenching properties but also as a source of nutrition. The brewing process left behind residual nutrients from the malted grains, providing a decent caloric intake for those who consumed it. This was especially valuable during times of scarcity and famine when food resources were limited.

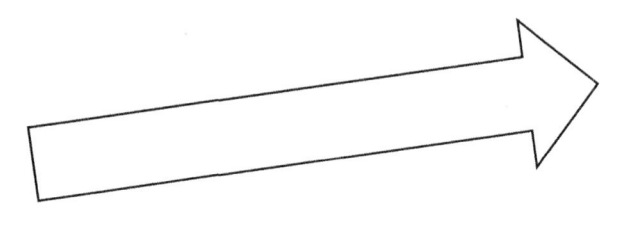

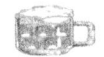

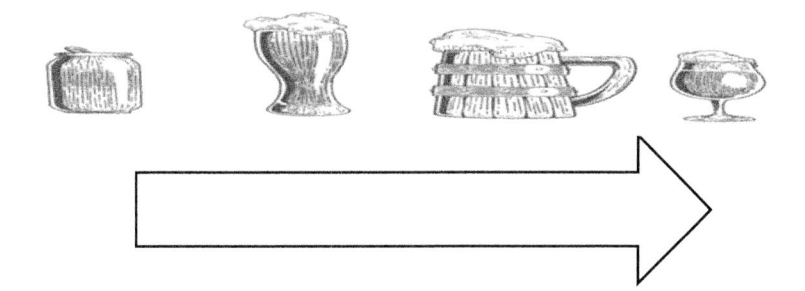

2. Brew to the Rescue

Thankfully, the brewing process of beer involved boiling water, which killed off harmful bacteria and parasites, making it a much safer option for consumption. As a result, beer became an essential part of the daily diet for people of all ages, from noble knights to merry peasants.

3. Monk Mastery

Monasteries became the bastions of brewing knowledge during this era. Monks, with their meticulous attention to detail and dedication, took brewing to new heights. Their brewing techniques involved heating the water, malting the grains, and adding hops for flavour and preservation. This meticulous process further ensured the elimination of harmful pathogens, making beer a reliable and safe beverage for hydration.

6. Drinking with Caution

Of course, it's worth mentioning that even though beer was a safer alternative to water, excessive consumption could still lead to its fair share of merriment and misadventure. Let's just say that some medieval bards might have composed their most humorous and outrageous tales after a few too many rounds of ale!

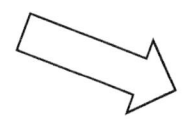

7. Conclusion

In a time when clean water was a luxury and hygiene standards were lacking, beer emerged as a saviour, providing a safer alternative for hydration. The brewing process, which involved boiling water and adding ingredients like hops, eliminated harmful pathogens and made beer a reliable and healthier alternative to untreated water sources. Beyond its practical benefits, beer also served as a social lubricant, bringing people together in laughter and camaraderie. So, raise your tankard to the medieval brewmasters and their frothy elixir, for they turned a potentially hazardous situation into a safer - and more entertaining - drinking experience. Cheers!

Every weekend I say "Bob, you've got to stop drinking."
Thankfully, my name's not Bob.

Know Thy Beer, Know Thy Self

Let's dive into the wonderful world of beer and explore some commonly available varieties, their brewing processes, and the type of men who might enjoy them. Sit back, relax, and let the beer knowledge flow!

Ales

Ales are the life and soul of the party—they're lively, energetic, and full of flavour. They're brewed with top-fermenting yeast that operates at warmer temperatures, resulting in a quicker fermentation process. This speedy transformation gives ales their characteristic fruity and sometimes spicy flavours. Ales range from pale ales with their hoppy bitterness to amber ales with their caramel maltiness. The type of man who enjoys ales is like a spontaneous adventurer, always up for a good time and ready to embrace bold flavours with a cheeky smile.

Lagers

Lagers are the cool, calm, and collected beers. They're brewed with bottom-fermenting yeast that works its magic at colder temperatures, resulting in a slower fermentation process. This extended fermentation gives lagers their crisp, clean taste and smooth finish. From pale lagers to the darker Munich dunkels, lagers cover a wide spectrum of flavours. The man who appreciates lagers is like the Zen master of beer, seeking a chilled-out experience, refined simplicity, and a beer that goes down smoothly.

Stouts

Ah, stouts—the dark, brooding rebels of the beer world. These beers are brewed using roasted malts, which gives them their deep, almost black colour and rich, robust flavours. With notes of coffee, chocolate, and sometimes even a touch of smokiness, stouts offer a complex and indulgent drinking experience. The man who gravitates towards stouts is like the strong, silent type—mysterious, yet with a deep appreciation for the finer things in life. He's the kind of guy who knows how to savour each sip and isn't afraid to embrace the darkness.

IPAs (India Pale Ales)

IPAs are the rebels with a hoppy cause. These beers are known for their intense hop bitterness and aromatic profiles. Whether it's the classic American IPA or the more tropical West Coast IPA, these beers pack a punch. IPAs are brewed with generous amounts of hops, which lend them their characteristic floral, citrusy, or piney flavours. The man who loves IPAs is like a hophead warrior, ready to conquer any challenge and embrace the bold bitterness with gusto. He's the guy who loves his beer with an extra dose of attitude.

Wheat Beers

Wheat beers are the friendly, approachable brews of the bunch. These beers are brewed with a significant proportion of wheat in addition to malted barley, resulting in a lighter and often cloudy appearance. With their refreshing and sometimes fruity flavours, wheat beers are perfect for quenching your thirst on a sunny day. The man who finds solace in wheat beers is like a laid-back dude who enjoys the simple pleasures in life. He's the kind of guy you'd want to share a beer with while kicking back in a hammock, swapping stories and soaking in the good vibes.

Pilsners

Pilsners are the sophisticated, refined beers that elevate any occasion. Originating from the Czech Republic, these beers are known for their pale golden colour, delicate malt flavours, and floral hop notes. Pilsners are traditionally bottom-fermented and undergo a lengthy cold maturation process, resulting in a beer that's crisp, clean, and perfectly balanced. The man who appreciates pilsners is the epitome of class and elegance. He knows how to appreciate the subtle nuances in life and enjoys the simple pleasure of a well-crafted beer.

Remember, these descriptions are all in good fun and should be taken with a grain of barley. The wide array of beer styles and the men who love them all have their own merits, each adding their own unique flavour to the beer-loving community!

"Always do sober what you said you'd do drunk. That will teach you to keep your mouth shut."
Ernest Hemingway

BEER FESTIVAL

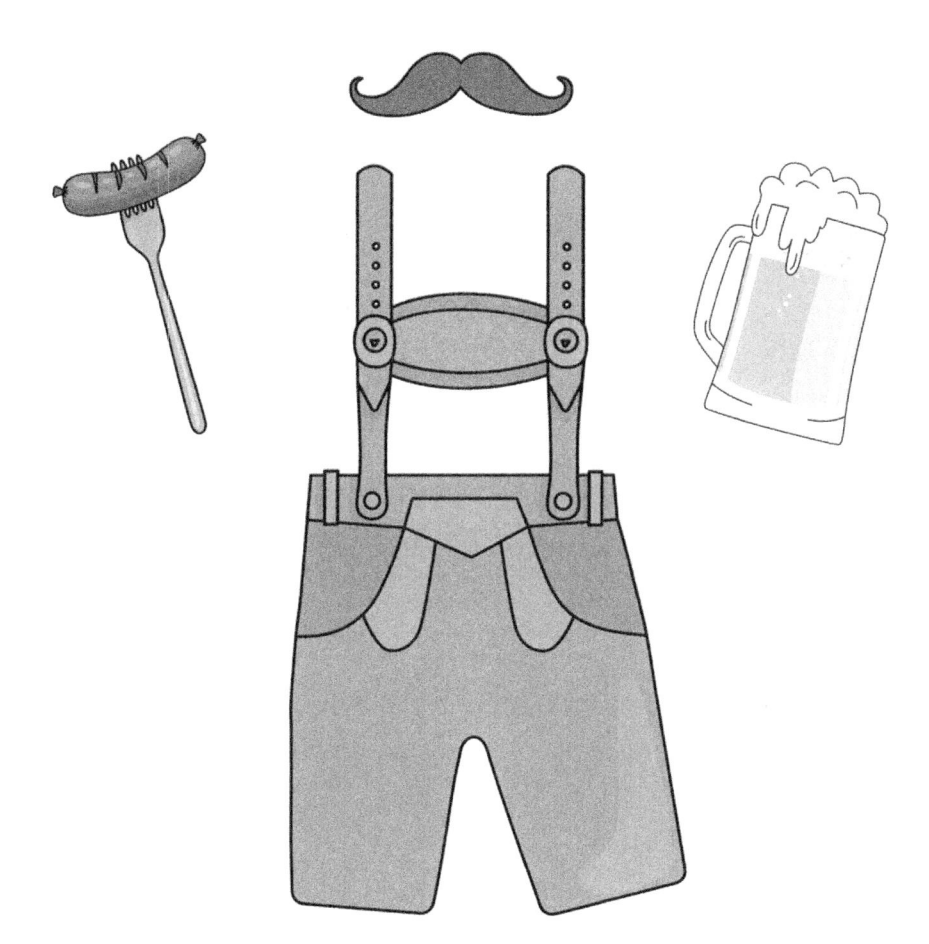

CUT OUT & KEEP OUTFIT*

*May be better suited for extremely small drinkers

Let's Get the Party Started!

Would you like to make your next beer drinking session more interesting? Here are ten popular and easy-to-play drinking games that can add a touch of fun to your next party, gathering, or session at the bar!

Beer Pong

A classic party game that involves throwing ping pong balls across a table with the aim of landing them in cups of beer. If the opponents ball lands in your cup, you drink its contents.

Flip Cup

This game requires two teams. Each person has a cup of beer, and they must drink it and then flip the cup upside down by flicking the rim with their fingers. The first team to finish and flip all their cups wins.

Kings

A card-based game where players take turns drawing cards from a deck with each card corresponding to a rule. For example, a "Queen" may mean that everyone must take a sip, while a "King" allows the person who drew the card to create a new rule.

Power Hour

Participants drink a shot of beer every minute for an hour. This game can be played with a timer or by using a specially created playlist with one-minute songs. Let's get to it!

Drunk Jenga

A twist on the classic game of Jenga. Each block has a rule written on it, such as "Take two sips" or "Make a rule." When a player removes a block, they must follow the corresponding rule.

Quarters

Players take turns bouncing a quarter (or 10p coin) off the table in an attempt to have it land in a cup of beer. If successful, the player can choose someone to drink.

Drunk Waiter

Participants balance a tray with shot glasses filled with various alcoholic beverages. The goal is to reach the finish line without dropping any glasses. If a glass falls, the player must drink its contents.

Never Have I Ever

Players take turns making statements starting with "Never have I ever..." Anyone who has done the mentioned action must take a drink. Get ready to reveal some interesting and potentially embarrassing secrets.

Roxanne

This game requires a song, usually "Roxanne" by The Police. Players drink every time the word "Roxanne" is mentioned in the song. Hopefully, this is the only police you sing to this evening!

Anchorman

Inspired by the movie "Anchorman," participants take turns quoting lines from the film. If someone fails to correctly quote a line or repeats a line, they must take a drink.

Remember to drink responsibly and be aware of your limits. Enjoy the fun!

A skeleton walks into a bar. He orders a beer... and a mop.

My Bucket List

✓ **BEER**

✓ **ICE**

✓ **BUCKET**

THE HANGOVER SURVIVAL KIT

Have you ever enjoyed that pounding head, nausea and dry mouth?

I thought not. Whether it's a stag or bucks do, beer festival, special occasion or big night out with friends – some occasions tend to go hand in hand with the types of hangover that feel like your brain is being squeezed in a vice.

Chances are that many beer enthusiasts have at some point felt the pain and discomfort that rears it's ugly head after a heavy session. But like any well-versed boy scout, the key is to 'Be prepared!'.

Fear not; whether you're suffering on a sofa, in a faraway hotel or cowering at home in bed. Pack this trusty hangover kit to ensure your faculties and headache free demeanour are swiftly restored and ready to head into Round Two.

- ❏ **Pepto Bismol or Alka Seltzer – to relieve upset stomachs**
- ❏ **Bottle of water**
- ❏ **Electrolyte packet**
- ❏ **Earplugs**
- ❏ **Gum or mints**
- ❏ **Aspirin, Ibuprofen or Paracetamol**
- ❏ **Tea or coffee**
- ❏ **Can of 'full fat' Coke (a personal favourite)**
- ❏ **Snacks – bananas, chocolate or granola bars in case you miss breakfast**
- ❏ **Sunglasses to hide your shame**
- ❏ **Eyedrops**
- ❏ **Vitamin C tablets**

HANGXIETY

-

A FEELING OF WORRY, UNEASE OR DREAD AFTER A HEAVY NIGHT OUT. ESPECIALLY WHERE THERE IS POOR RECOLLECTION OVER EVENTS THAT OCCURRED.

Charlie Chaplin's Cocktail Caper

The comedic genius of silent film, Charlie Chaplin, was once invited to a grand cocktail party at a lavish mansion. Known for his slapstick humour, Chaplin couldn't resist playing a prank or two on his fellow guests. Seizing an opportunity when the bartender wasn't looking, he swapped the contents of various liquor bottles with absurd concoctions he had prepared earlier. Champagne mixed with pickle juice, vodka infused with hot sauce, and whiskey spiked with a hint of vinegar became the drinks of the evening. As the unsuspecting guests took their first sips, chaos erupted. People gagged, sputtered, and desperately tried to cleanse their palates with whatever was at hand. Chaplin, hidden in the corner, laughed uncontrollably at his mischievous masterpiece, ensuring that his reputation as a prankster was solidified.

Cheers!

Consider yourself a worldly beer drinker? Here are 50 of the biggest beer brands in the world. Tick off all the ones you've tried and get a bonus point if you can answer which country they come from. Check your marks out of 100 - answers on page 72.

	Beer	**Country of Origin**		**Beer**	**Country of Origin**
❑	San Miguel	....	❑	Antarctica	....
❑	Cristal	....	❑	Carlsberg	....
❑	Super Bock	....	❑	Pilsner Urquell	....
❑	Zubr	....	❑	Estrella	....
❑	Cruzcampo	....	❑	Tiger	....
❑	Becks	....	❑	Victoria	....
❑	Peroni	....	❑	Stella Artois	....
❑	Yanjing	....	❑	Leffe	....
❑	Samuel Adams	....	❑	Red Stripe	....
❑	Chang	....	❑	Brahma	....
❑	Carling	....	❑	Tecate	....
❑	Fosters	....	❑	Harbin	....
❑	Kronenbourg	....	❑	Michelob	....
❑	Kingfisher	....	❑	Tsingtao	....
❑	Aguila	....	❑	Guinness	....
❑	Desperados	....	❑	Miller Lite	....
❑	Castle	....	❑	Kirin	....
❑	Zhujiang	....	❑	Asahi	....
❑	Cass	....	❑	Coors	....
❑	Dos Equis XX	....	❑	Snow	....
❑	Natural	....	❑	Modelo Especial	....
❑	Mahou	....	❑	Brewdog Punk IPA	....
❑	Saigon	....	❑	Budweiser	....
❑	Tuborg	....	❑	Heineken	....
❑	Mythos	....	❑	Corona	....

SPILLING A FULL GLASS OF BEER IS THE ADULT EQUIVALENT OF LETTING GO OF A BALLOON

THE BEER DICTIONARY

BEER JACKET
The economical way to stay warm on a cold night. Once beers have been consumed, the wearer of this invisible layer is immune to the cold on the 2am walk home.

BEER GOGGLES
Allows the wearer to view any potential objects of affection in their most flattering light. Beware: the effect may wear off the following morning.

BEER-DAR
The user can sense the nearest pub or bar within a 1,000-metre radius to start or continue consumption.

COULDN'T ARRANGE A PISSUP IN A BREWERY
Considered useless and incompetent. Organisational qualities held in the lowest regard.

BEER COMPASS
Safely navigates you home after many beers, even if upon reflection you are unable to remember the journey.

BEER ARMOUR
An invisible shield that allows the wearer to feel no pain when inebriated.

BEER O'CLOCK
The time of day to start drinking beer. Can be used flexibly to validate the user's decision to start drinking, or as a mutual decision to stop working and go to the pub.

CHEEKY BEER
A last minute or unplanned chance to have a beer with a friend or colleague.

BEER POO
A turd brewed in the bowels of Satan himself. Known to appear the morning after a heavy session one or more times. Jet-black in appearance, it's known to leave your ass red raw and requires copious amounts of toilet roll.

ROAD BEER
A beer to enjoy on a journey to more beers. E.g. I took a road beer on the train.

The World's Best Beer Snacks

Sometimes we're forced to pause our beer drinking fun and refuel to keep our stamina up! If you can't decide what to have for your next beer snack, here are some of the world's tastiest to look out for when hunger strikes.

Pretzels (Germany)

Nutritional Benefits: Pretzels are a beer-lover's dream come true! They're salty, crunchy, and rich in carbohydrates, providing a perfect beer-absorbing base. Carbs give you that quick energy boost to keep the party going, and the salt helps prevent dehydration (aka "the morning after" woes!). Plus, their twisted shape mirrors our feelings when we can't get enough beer and snacks!

Nachos (Mexico)

Nutritional Benefits: Ole! Nachos are the fiesta of beer snacks! These cheesy, crispy tortilla chips topped with mouthwatering goodness like guacamole, salsa, and melted cheese, are a guaranteed crowd-pleaser. The avocados in guac bring the good kind of fats, while the salsa provides a punch of vitamins. They're a sombrero wearing treat for your taste buds!

Tempura Shrimp (Japan)

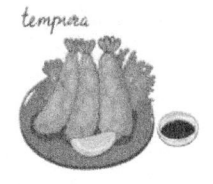

Nutritional Benefits: Konnichiwa! These beer-battered taste sensations are the yin to your beer's yang. Not only are they delicious, but they're also a great source of protein, giving you the strength to power through more drinks with your buddies. The crispy coating adds a satisfying crunch, making them a beer lover's go to Japanese snack.

Poutine (Canada)

Nutritional Benefits: Oh, Canada! The Great White North brings us the comforting and oh-so-satisfying poutine. Fries drenched in cheese curds and gravy might not be the healthiest, but they're a must-have indulgence. The cheese curds offer a delightful burst of calcium, keeping your bones strong and your taste buds fulfilled.

Chicharrones (Mexico and Latin America)

Nutritional Benefits: Say "hola" to chicharrones, the crispy, crunchy, and oh-so-addictive fried pork skins! These savoury treats are packed with protein, perfect for balancing out the beer's liquid happiness. They may not be the healthiest snack on the block, but when it comes to satisfying beer cravings, they're top-notch!

Tapas (Spain)

Nutritional Benefits: Ole! Spanish tapas are a tantalising assortment of small bites, perfect for beer lovers who crave variety. From chorizo to olives to patatas bravas, these bite-sized wonders offer a mix of flavours and textures. Olives deliver heart-healthy fats, while patatas bravas provide potassium to keep your electrolytes happy as you continue your beer adventure!

Samosas (India)

Nutritional Benefits: Namaste! Samosas, those crispy, triangular pockets filled with spiced goodness, are an Indian delight that pairs perfectly with beer. The vegetable fillings, like potatoes and peas, offer a dose of fibre and vitamins. So, enjoy these little flavour explosions while adding some nutritional magic to your beer session!

Mozzarella Sticks (Italy)

Nutritional Benefits: Ciao! Mozzarella sticks, those gooey, golden goodies, are an Italian-American invention that won the hearts of beer lovers everywhere. They provide a delightful calcium boost from the cheese, helping to balance out the brew's dehydrating effects. Dip them in marinara sauce, and you've got a match made in beer-snack heaven!

Biltong (South Africa)

Nutritional Benefits: Howzit! Biltong, South Africa's answer to jerky, is a protein-packed snack with a unique blend of flavours. Made from air-dried beef or game meats, biltong is low in fat and high in essential nutrients, like iron and zinc. So, chew on these South African delights while you raise a glass to the spirit of adventure!

Chicken Wings (United States)

Nutritional Benefits: Finger-lickin' good! Chicken wings are an all-American beer snack favourite. Whether they're slathered in spicy Buffalo sauce or coated in tangy barbecue, they satisfy our taste buds like no other. The protein in wings provides the strength to lift your beer mug with gusto and keep the beer-loving spirit alive!

So, grab your favourite beer, pick your snack partner in crime, and embark on a flavour-filled journey of good times and belly laughs! Cheers, amigos.

Beer Anagrams

Take a close look around your humble surroundings. The jumbled words below are items related to beer and places it is commonly consumed – fill in the gaps and see how many points you can get out of 20. Answers on page 73.

1. Laborsto = ...
2. Regal = ...
3. Weberry = ...
4. Salgs = ...
5. Lea = ...
6. Entirefanmot = ...
7. Tribet = ...
8. Staye = ...
9. Rebral = ...
10. Inset = ...
11. Shop = ...
12. Nitp = ...
13. Anvert = ...
14. Aportom = ...
15. Ambraid = ...
16. Sack = ...
17. Kurdn = ...
18. Purcawlb = ...
19. Ekg = ...
20. Mabreet = ...

Why is sex on a boat like Mexican beer? Both are fucking close to water.

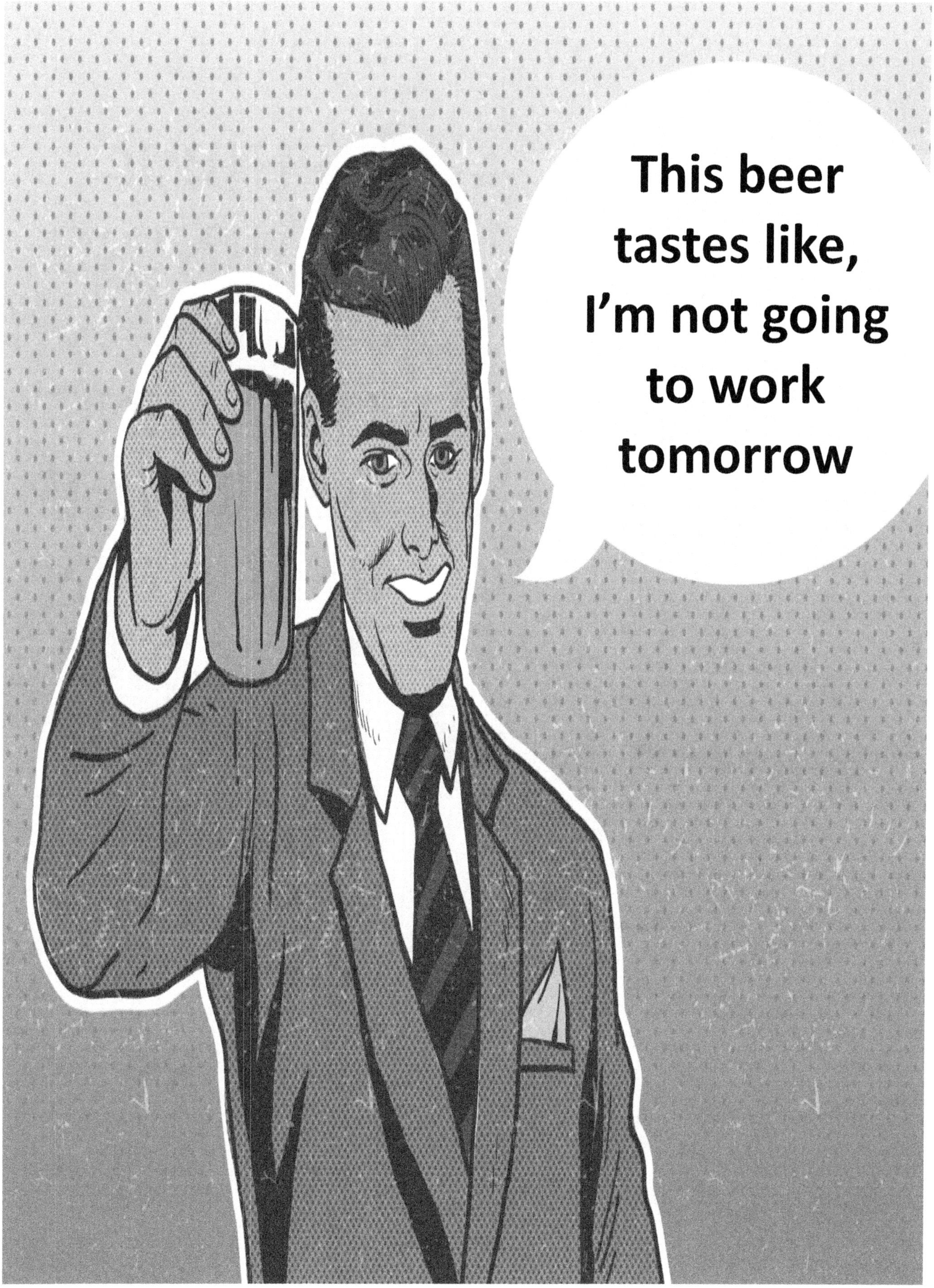
This beer tastes like, I'm not going to work tomorrow

PUBLIC WARNING -

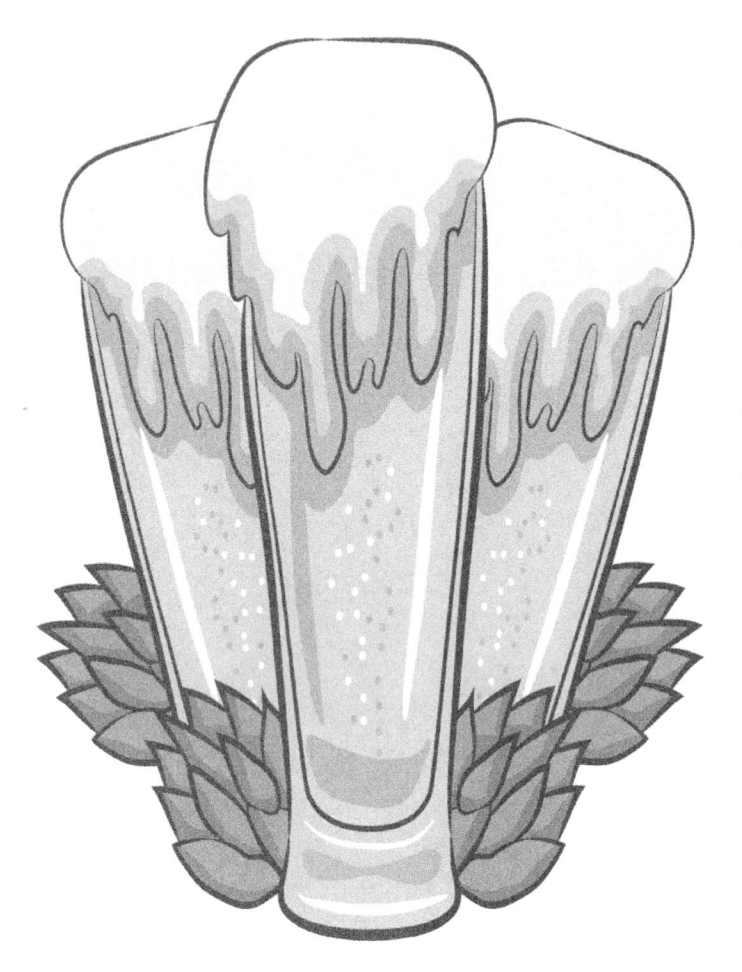

DRINKING BEER MAY RESULT IN MEMORY LOSS, OR WORSE STILL MEMORY LOSS

What goes up must come down!

Or if you've really overshot the mark, what goes down sometimes comes up! Whether it's a dodgy pint, an unfamiliar ABV or the temptation of just one more – sometimes our favourite beverage can lead to an unsightly hangover. Never fear gentleman, here are some battle tested hangover cures to straighten out that sore head of yours quicker than you can say 'next round!'

The Breakfast of Champions: Chow down on a feast fit for a king! Pancakes, bacon, eggs or a good old fashioned British fry-up – pile it on to soak up the night's excesses. The combination of carbs and grease will brighten you up in no time!

The Hair of the Dog: Why suffer today, when you can push the pain back until tomorrow? The recourse of the brave or the reckless, when the going gets tough, the tough go back to the source! It's like fighting fire with...well, more firewater!

The Ninja Nap: Sneak in a stealthy power nap between morning meetings. You can claim it's a strategic productivity technique, but we all know it's your secret hangover recovery strategy!

The Disco Shower: Turn up the music, and let the shower bring you back to life! Dance away your hangover worries and emerge fresh and revitalised.

The Appliance of Science: As a diuretic, too much of the good stuff can easily lead to dehydration. Drink plenty of water before, during and after your beer adventure to stave off the headaches and dizziness. Add some electrolytes (such as calcium, magnesium and sodium) and light exercise for good measure to get yourself back on top form.

The Comedy Marathon: Sometimes laughter is the best medicine. Take refuge in bed or your favourite chair, queue up your back catalogue of sitcoms or stand-up specials, and let the laughter wash away the hangover blues!

The Ancient Elixir: Sometimes the old remedies are the best. Seek out the old family recipe – an elixir that promises to cure all ills. It might taste bizarre, but hey, desperate times call for desperate measures!

Good luck gentleman. Enjoy your drinks responsibly and may your hangovers be fleeting as you continue your beer-loving adventures!

MORE BEER TRIVIA

The US state of Colorado has the highest number of breweries per capita in the country.

The fear of running out of beer is known as cenosillicaphobia, striking terror into the heart of every beer lover.

The term 'session beer' relates to a beer with a lower alcohol content – normally ranging between 3.5-5% - that can be consumed over longer drinking sessions.

In 1959, beer cans with pull ring tabs were introduced which revolutionised beer packaging at the time.

Beer is thought to have played a role in the invention of bread. The fermentation process is linked to the discovery of leavened bread.

The world's oldest operating brewery is a former Benedictine Monastery located in Germany, dating back to at least 1040.

- ODE TO THE PUB -

If beer was a religion, then surely the pub would be the beer lovers place of worship. Kneel at the alter of refreshment, and give thanks as we dive into the humble history of the sacred place we call the pub.

The Pub: Where Beer and Brotherhood Come Together

Gather round gentleman! As we head to the sacred realm of the pub, its important to acknowledge the significance of this unique location. A pub is not just a place; but a right of passage. A sanctuary of socialising and camaraderie that greets you with open arms to serve you with your favourite tipple.

-

So, grab a cold one, and let's unravel the epic tale of the iconic public house.

Chapter 1: The Pub - A Brief History Lesson

Ah, the pub, short for "public house." Its roots run deep, back to the time when kings and commoners shared a pint in merry unison. Imagine yourself transported to ancient Mesopotamia, where the world's first brewers concocted their liquid gold. Fast forward through the ages, and you'll find yourself drinking ales in the lively taverns of medieval Europe.

-

The pub has always been more than just a place to quench one's thirst. It's a focal point of the local community and a hub of human connection. A place to pull up a chair and swap epic tales of adventure, to unwind or to whisper in the shadowy corners of revolutionary plans.

Chapter 2: The Anatomy of a Pub

Picture your typical pub. A place with dim lighting, wooden furnishings and an assortment of pictures and knick-knacks hanging from the walls.

Quiet corners and cosy booths. Long wooden tables for raucous gatherings. Bar stools for the solo contemplative drinkers and an atmosphere of warmth, laughter and good conversation.

-

The occasional pub game and of course, the focal point – the bar. Manned by the bartender; part friend, part enforcer and part therapist. These lynchpins of the public house are the gatekeepers to the divine nectar; the engine that keeps this glorious machine running smoothly. Always keep the bartender on side, and soon they'll be pouring your favourite tipple for you as soon as you walk through the doors!

Chapter 3: The Beer - Nectar of the Pub Gods

The pièce de résistance is of course, the beer! In the pub, it's not just a beverage; it's a passport to adventure. From the crisp lagers that greet you like an old friend, to the complex ales that beckon you like sultry sirens. The pub's beer menu is a treasure trove begging to be explored.

-

"Give me your finest IPA," you'll declare as you peruse the menu, only to be overwhelmed by the vast selection on offer. The bartender, with the wisdom of an ancient sage, guides you to your destiny like an expert marksman. Take comfort that you are amongst friends. Savour and enjoy the nectar of the gods as it refreshes and rejuvenates your spirit.

Chapter 4: The Pub Fare - A Feast for the Ages

Now, let's not forget the pub fare, the hearty sustenance that fuels our beer-fuelled escapades. Pub food is a culinary journey designed to compliment your brew, from the classics like fish and chips to more exotic offerings like gourmet burgers with toppings that could make a food critic weep.

-

And then there are the snacks - peanuts, crisps, and pickled eggs – humble yet strangely addictive. Serving as the perfect accompaniment to your pint, the pubs assortment of snacks reminds us that sometimes, simplicity is the key to success.

Chapter 5: The Pub Regulars - A Brotherhood in Ale

Ah, the regulars! Every pub has them – the familiar faces who occupy the same stool, night after night. They're the unsung heroes of the pub, keeping its spirit alive. They'll regale you with tales of yesteryears, share sage-like advice, and offer recommendations of the best brews available.

-

Becoming a regular is like joining an exclusive club, and the pub is your clubhouse. It's a place where friendships are forged, and where, occasionally, you'll find yourself in spirited debates over the finest lagers and stouts, as if the fate of the world depended on it.

Chapter 6: Pub Games - Where Fun Meets Fermentation

A pub without games is like a beer without bubbles - incomplete. Whether it's a classic game of darts or a nail-biting pool match, these games are the spice of pub life. They're an excuse to test your skills, challenge your pals, and, of course, buy a round for the winner.

-

And let's not forget the legendary pub quiz nights, where trivia titans battle for supremacy over pints and snacks. Beware the "know-it-all" who secretly googles the answers; they're the modern-day villains of the pub quiz circuit.

Chapter 7: Closing Time - A Bittersweet Farewell

Alas, all good things must come to an end, and so does the night at the pub. Closing time looms like a mythical beast as the bell for last orders echoes through its walls. You may squeeze one last one in before drinking up and bidding adieu to your newfound friends and empty glasses. The street outside is plain and grey in comparison, without the warmth and vibrancy the pub offers.

-

But fear not, for the pub will always be there, waiting with open arms and frothy pints for your return. Offering a steadfast friend, confidante, and home away from home for weary travellers and thirsty locals alike.

To conclude, my dear beer-loving brethren, the pub is not just a place; it's an experience. Standing as a testament to the enduring appeal of good company, great beer, and the timeless tradition of raising a glass to life's ups and downs. So, next time you step into your favourite local watering hole, raise your glass high and toast to the pub, where beer and brotherhood converge in a symphony of joy. Amen to that!

Alongside their unique heritage and appeal, pubs also have an array of weird and wonderful names. Here are the 10 most popular names from the UK – look out for these as a sign of cold beer and a warm welcome:

- The Red Lion
- The Royal Oak
- New Inn
- The Crown Inn
- The White Hart
- The Rose & Crown
- The White Horse
- The Kings Arms
- The Plough
- The George

Beer World Records – Part 2

The record for the most beer bottles opened in a minute currently stands at 110!

The largest stack of beer mats – or coasters – flipped and caught was 112! It took the new champion Mat Hand of the UK over 4 hours and 129 attempts to beat the old record of 111 beer mats.

The world record for the highest beer keg toss was 7.75 metres or 25'6" by American strongman Brian Shaw. The beer keg thrown weighed 33 pounds or 15kg.

HOW TO ORDER
BEER
AROUND THE WORLD

BIRA ONEGAI SHIMASU
- JAPAN -

UNA BIRRA, PER FAVORE
- ITALY -

BIR BIRA LUTFEN
- TURKEY -

UNE BIERE, S'IL VOUS PLAIT
- FRANCE -

A BEER, PLEASE!
- UK/USA -

EIN BIER, BITTE
- GERMANY -

YED-NO PEEV, PROSHE!
- POLAND -

UNA CERVEZA, POR FAVOUR
- SPAIN -

PIA, HO'OLU!
- HAWAIIAN -

PEE-VO, PRO-SEEM!
- CZECH REPUBLIC -

A BEER, ZEIT A-ZUY GOOT
- YIDDISH -

EEN BIER, ALSJEBLIEFT
- HOLLAND -

'N BIER, ASSEBLIEF
- SOUTH AFRICA -

"O'zapft is!"

"O'zapft is! – A Bavarian saying and call that signifies the start of Oktoberfest!

Meaning 'the beer is tapped' – without this phrase Oktoberfest doesn't start and you don't get your beer and pretzels!

TREAT YOUR LIFE AND BEER THE SAME

CHILL FOR BEST RESULTS

Cheers! - Answers

Consider yourself a worldly beer drinker? See the beers below and which country they came from to give yourself a mark out of 100.

	Beer	Country of Origin		Beer	Country of Origin
❑	San Miguel	Spain	❑	Antarctica	Brazil
❑	Cristal	Chile	❑	Carlsberg	Denmark
❑	Super Bock	Portugal	❑	Pilsner Urquell	Czech Republic
❑	Zubr	Poland	❑	Estrella	Spain
❑	Cruzcampo	Spain	❑	Tiger	Singapore
❑	Becks	Germany	❑	Victoria	Mexico
❑	Peroni	Italy	❑	Stella Artois	Belgium
❑	Yanjing	China	❑	Leffe	Belgium
❑	Samuel Adams	USA	❑	Red Stripe	Jamaica
❑	Chang	Thailand	❑	Brahma	Brazil
❑	Carling	Canada	❑	Tecate	Mexico
❑	Fosters	Australia	❑	Harbin	China
❑	Kronenbourg	France	❑	Michelob	USA
❑	Kingfisher	India	❑	Tsingtao	China
❑	Aguila	Colombia	❑	Guinness	Ireland
❑	Desperados	France	❑	Miller Lite	USA
❑	Castle	South Africa	❑	Kirin	Japan
❑	Zhujiang	China	❑	Asahi	Japan
❑	Cass	South Korea	❑	Coors	USA
❑	Dos Equis XX	Mexico	❑	Snow	China
❑	Natural	USA	❑	Modelo Especial	Mexico
❑	Mahou	Spain	❑	Brewdog Punk IPA	Scotland
❑	Saigon	Vietnam	❑	Budweiser	USA
❑	Tuborg	Denmark	❑	Heineken	Holland
❑	Mythos	Greece	❑	Corona	Mexico

Answer Page

Anagram answers – page 58:

1. Barstool
2. Lager
3. Brewery
4. Glass
5. Ale
6. Fermentation
7. Bitter
8. Yeast
9. Barrel
10. Stein
11. Hops
12. Pint
13. Tavern
14. Taproom
15. Barmaid
16. Cask
17. Drunk
18. Pubcrawl
19. Keg
20. Beermat

If you enjoyed this fun filled romp through the glorious world of beer, make sure you checkout I.P Freely's runaway hit 'The Ultimate Toilet Activity Book'. The perfect accompaniment for those long trips to the loo or as a gift for those hard to buy for friends or relatives:

'The Ultimate Toilet Activity Book'.

Just use the QR code above to take you straight to the book!

Thank you!

Just a note to say thank you for buying this book. We hope you loved reading it as much as we loved writing about all thing's beer!

If you enjoyed the book, please consider leaving us a review on Amazon to help us keep creating more books that you'll love.

Printed in Great Britain
by Amazon